For Val

A Woeful Tale

from

Derrick Cranpole

Dranpole

Dunmore East

First Published in 2012 by The Manuscript Publisher

ISBN: 978-0-9571157-1-2

A CIP Catalogue record for this book is available from the British Library

Cover design by Christine

Typesetting and page layout by DocumentsandManuscripts.com

Contents

FISHERMEN MUST PULL TOGETHER

1

A WOEFUL TAIL

Two Bogey Men flom Department of Maline
Walk into my plemmises quite unseen
They sit at a table ask for Robster and Wine
They have Robster, Water Chestnuts, Flied Lice
velly fine

They eat Water Chestnuts and the flied lice too
They dlink up the wine and say "Coffee for two"
But when I fetch them coffee they say "We have
News for you!
We put a measure on the Robsters and one of
them did fail
The other one he big enough but have V notch in
the tail!
I say "Oh I velly solly but you see in Old Hong
Kong
Robsters they are rittle in fact about this rong
And rittle Chinese Robsters born with V notch in
their tails
Just like Chinese dragons, Chinese newts and
even Chinese snails.

The Bogey Men they rook at me with Occidental eyes
They say that I am terring naughty Oliental ries
They say "Thankyou for the Robsters"
They say "Thankyou for the wine"
They say "If you not go to Plison you get broody whacking fine!"

It is illegal to possess a lobster that has a V notch cut in its tail fin, or indeed a damaged tail fin. Great!
Almost nobody knows this, or that the minimum size measured from behind the eye to the back of the carapace of the lobster is 87mm. Watch out for that when you order Lobster Thermidor!

2

REMEMBER

Remember when we fished in oilskins shiny -red?
We fished by day and fished by night
And hardly ever went to bed.

Up and down the nets for ever steaming
Watching, ever watching for the salmon scales
 a'gleaming
And then one strikes! Look lively now
The dipping headline cork's just o'er her bow
A burst of speed, then give her starboard wheel
Snatch up the Salmon to cheat the cunning Seal

Ah those were happy days. No Dole back then
But proud we were to be Ireland's Fishermen.

But now, by Legislation badly flawed
Small boat fishermen have been outlawed
And its all been done by Politics
And Lobbying and clever Tricks
And the Fishermen are caught between
Smart Anglers and misguided Green

So must we say a sad farewell
To the men and boys (some girls as well)
Who fished in oilskins shiny red
By day and night and hardly ever went to bed
And in small boats with tiny mizzens set
Followed ever
Followed the drifting Salmon net.

The Salmon drift net ban was not unexpected due to pressure from the powerful angling and tourism interests. We are still in trouble over the EU water quality directive. Every lake river and stream in Ireland is polluted but the Ban proves that we are good little conservation minded Europeans.

3

TOXIC DUMP

The answer to pollution is dilution
So if you've got something nasty on your mind
You can dump it in the sea
Which is absolutely free
And toxic mud is very hard to find
Oh yes toxic mud is very hard to find

Now whoever gives a damn for a mussel or a clam
A herring or a codfish or a dab
And not many people feel any feelings for an eel
And who likes shaking hands with any crab?
If you want to save the planet
Every kittiwake and gannet
Then write to the Department of Marine
In their offices secure their environment is pure
And their attitudes are positively green
They will say, dear friends relax kindly do not
write or fax
For the toxic mud we have the perfect cure

We put the mud into a ship and we send it on a
trip
And we dump it where the silver fishes dart

Where the shrimps are all alive and where soaring gannets dive
But it's empty sea according to our chart
Just trust that our solution to pollution is dilution
And if you have something nasty on your mind
You can dump it in the sea
Which is absolutely free
And toxic mud is very hard to find
Oh yes toxic mud is very hard to find.

"SHAKE HANDS ANYONE?"

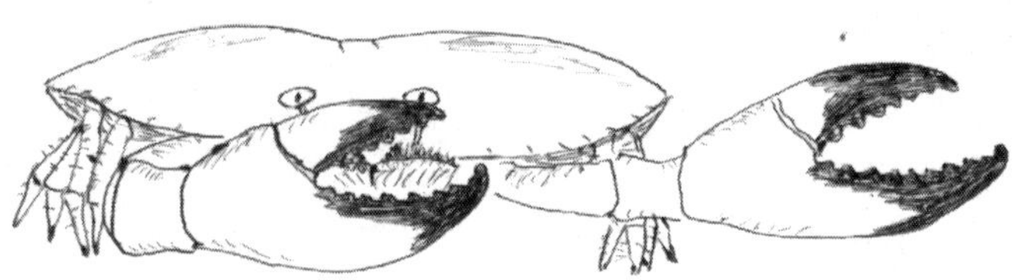

4

THE QUALIFIED MAN

I've been to Greencastle
I've been through the hassle
I'm a Cookie
I'm a Deckie
I'm a Second Hand Special

I've done "Sea Survival" and "Fighting of Fires"
I've practised "Net Mending" and "Splicing of Wires"

And I've done my best
To pass every test
That "Safe Operation of Vessels" requires.

So how can it be
That when I go to Sea
There's a mountainy man on the Deck next to me
He can't take a watch and he just doesn't care
He can't fill a needle yet he gets a full share.

Now something is wrong I don't care who's to blame
I'm not sticking this for the love of the game.

I'd be far better off with a job on the Shore
With bonuses earned on the Factory Floor
Where people are paid according to grade
And enjoy the rewards of learning their trade.

All those lads who gave up their fishing time and paid for these courses, run by BIM are treated the same as a complete landlubber.

5

THE POOR RELATIONS

In Nineteen Hundred and Ninety Eight
B.I.M. was told to investigate
The Inshore Fisheries of the state.
And find out whatever is wrong - oh

So away they went with paper and pen
Intelligent women, and experienced men
Asking Fisher folk the where and the when
And their lists grew ever so long - oh

Through Wexford and Youghal round to North
  Donegal
They visited Harbours both mighty and small
And they called in at places with no Pier at all
And recorded the same sorry song - oh

The result was a glossy and bright magazine
With figures and graphs explaining the scene
And pictures and photos as fine as we've seen
But we don't need a Doctor or Don - oh

To tell of neglect and bitter frustration
Official deceit and the Fleets decimation

Our Industry now is a shame on the Nation
Yet the economy is ever so strong - oh

(Best sung to a slow air and backed by a solitary
Bong - oh)

Yet another expensive survey to tell us what we already know

6

THE SANDS OF TIME

There's plenty of gravel in Cavan
And there's more in the County Kildare
And there's much more beneath
The Green hills of Meath
And in Eskers from Carlow to Clare

So why send out Dredgers to rip the Seabed?
Like everyone else they should buy sand instead
Why sanction destruction
By dredging and suction
Laying waste to the Ocean and leaving it dead?

Haven't they heard of Sediment Migration?
Surely our Seabed belongs to the Nation.
By stealing the sands
And denuding the Strands
They leave only the rocks to the next Generation

Yes, buy sand from the land if Developers need
To build houses and roads at remarkable speed
But we shouldn't mention

For fear of contention
That some people's actions are driven by greed.

A vessel came taking samples of the sea bed sands and gravels. We objected. The Minister of the Marine quite “lost the crust” at a meeting with us, “You can’t stop the industrialization of the river” he thundered “You are only lucky we don’t harvest the boulders!”

7

HELLO TIGER

The Celtic Tiger's been good to me
So I took early redundancy
And embarked on a life that's wild and free
Haul away me Boyos

I bought me a boat. She's not very old
She went for a song 'cos her tonnage was sold
And there's plenty of room below in her hold
Haul away me Boyos

She's horsepower a'plenty but no Kilowatts
When I give her the wellie she goes at ten knots
And now I've invested in six hundred pots
Haul away me Boyos

I see the lobstermen, thick as two planks
Returning small lobsters while I'm saying
"Thanks"
Soon I will have them in my storing tanks!
Haul away me Boyos

For me and my vessel Opportunity's knocking
Lobsters with notches are returned for restocking

And some days I catch them in numbers quite shocking
Haul away me Boyos

About the Department? Don't make me laugh
No Fishery Officer crosses my path
I am too cute and they haven't the staff
They're all away me Boyos.

So many boats were left fishing with no Registration by fishery Officers who turned a "blind eye", while others were picked on and forced to comply

8

EQUAL ACCESS I
or Bye Bye P.J.

Hey, Paddy Joe as off you go out on the Briny sea
To hunt the fish as father did
A sailing wild and free
Now don't you be the least concerned
If money's lost or money's earned
Or decommissioned boats are burned
Within the E.E.C.

Look Paddy Joe you really know that you are inefficient
We can swap this fleet of little boats,
Ten big ones are sufficient
We can help you with retraining
For a job that is sustaining
Or spend your time remaining
On the Dole.

Oh Paddy Joe give up the sea, Oh why get into debt
Give up toiling on the water
In the freezing cold and wet
We can train you as a Waiter

Or Computer Operator.
As a Pest Exterminator
You won't even need a net.

Oh Paddy Joe, as you must know, time's running
 out for you
Its much too late the final date
Is year two thousand two
When Europe's fleet come to our shore
Where you and father fished before
Your little boat will fish no more
Goodbye to you, its sad but true
Goodbye Paddy Joe.

April 1998

The EU proposal/intention was that EU fleets would be able to fish right up to the shore in 2002.

9

THE MANDARINS

We're the Mandarins of Leeson Lane
And from our Ivory Tower
We control the Fishing Fleet
And enjoy unlimited power
Maybe our system is arcane
And our methods out of date
And if at times we seem insane
Then Fishermen must appreciate
That Ministers come and Ministers go
We might say "yes" but we mean "No No"
And without needing to be clever
We Mandarins are here for ever
(And ever and ever).

At a meeting with him in Leinster House, the Minister promised us that we would have the individual Lobster Fishing Licences we sought. Afterwards, in the corridor outside, the Civil Servants assured us that it wouldn't happen. They were right. It didn't!

10

THE GURDEY MEN

Paddy was the Mackerel King
Of that there's no denying
Yet many tried to take his Crown
But had to give up trying.

Oh they tried it with Hydraulics
And from boats that were much bigger
And with fancy electronics
And an automatic jigger

But they could not match the Mackerel King
For expertise and cunning
Though many were quite good at it
They just weren't in the running

They put nine boxes on the floor
They thought that they had won
Then Paddy landed half a score
That's nearly half a ton!

Year in year out that's how it went
Until that fateful morn

When Paddy sniffed the mackerel scent
Out in the summer dawn

He steamed towards the sunrise
And suddenly he cursed
For a sneaky Geriatric
Had reached the mackerel first

Paddy raced toward the shoal
He was so intent on winning
With knotty little muscles
He sent his gurdy spinning

But the old guy he was razor keen
And he knew the finer points
And mackerel piled up round his knees
Despite arthritic joints

All day long the battle raged
Until the darkness fell
The boats raced back into the dock
Their catches for to sell

Well Paddy he was trembling
And his face betrayed his fear
As boxes full of mackerel
Were winched up on the pier

At last they could be counted
And at the final tally
Paddy was top by half a box
And he felt his spirits rally

Well Paddy got to bed at last
But he woke up with a start
With mackerel dancing round his bed
And terror struck his heart

His wife she wakened at his cries
And of course she knew the crack
She'd often been through this before
So she gently rubbed his back

"Oh Pat" says she "Go back to sleep
Don't be a silly thing
Don't get yourself up in a heap
You're still the Mackerel King!"

There was fierce competition amongst the Mackerel men and Paddy was usually "Top Boat".

11

A FISHERMAN'S FAREWELL.

Is it Bye, Bye Emma B?
Will you promise us you're going?
Are you flying out from Brussels
On a Tri star or a Boeing?

Let us hope your passing hurts
Those Fishing Bureaucrats
Who have hid behind your skirts.
And will they bail out like rats
Now your Ship of State is sinking
Now there's no one at the pumps
And the Commission's name is stinking.

Oh yes dear Emma B
When you fly back to Iberia
Will you take the C.F.P.?
And stuff it up the Interior.

Fisheries Commissioner Emma Bonino was leaving (and no harm either). According to newspaper reports there was something lacking in the Commission's accounting system around that time.

12

EQUAL ACCESS II or Welcome Pablo

Has that punt been Registered?
Does it have its Kilowatts?
And that little old half decker
Which only does five knots
Does it have a fishing licence
A polyvalent one?
This isn't simply nonsense
We account for every tonne!

All these targets must be met
To suit the C.F.P.
Before you ever shoot a net
Then Licensed you must be.
In this Common fishing Policy
The sea's for us to share
It's simply not codology
And it's absolutely fair.

So if you meet a Spanish ship
Just outside twelve mile
Then wish him a successful trip
And greet him with a smile

And don't be getting in his way
'Cos there's fourteen in his crew
But according to the C.F.P.
He's just the same as you.

More about small boats being pressured by the dept. of the Marine and the Navy, while others are free to do as they please. Spanish and other foreign vessels seem to operate outside the law within our waters.

13

A QUESTION OF KILOWATTS

"And what, tell me what, is a kilowatt?"
Says me man in the A.I.B.
Says I, "It replaces Horsepower
Since we joined the E.E.C.
And some boats do have Kilowatts
While other boats do not
And Kilowatts they're costly
At two hundred pounds a shot."

The Manager stroked his greying beard
And my fate hung by a thread
"That's the silliest yarn I've ever heard"
Imperiously he said
But I was bold and I was young
Blest with a voice of honey
And when he heard my silver tongue
He authorised the money.

So I bought my 20 kilowatts
From Mickey Joe next door
I thought he charged an awful lot
But he could have charged me more
For that 5 tons he sold me

From his ageing motor boat.
I thought she'd be retired from sea
But I see she's still afloat

Yes Mickey Joe's still fishing
And he's doing very well
His boat's no longer registered
And that's the truth to tell
Now he doesn't need a survey
Or need fire fighting gear
Nor the checking up on safety
To be repeated every year

But there's something that he does have
And this I really hate
A shiny big Mercedes
With this year's number plate.

Some Skippers were forced to borrow money to pay for kilowatts and tonnage at enormous expense, while some sold their tonnage and fished away without let or hindrance.

14

RIVER OF NO RETURN

Think of the Tisza River when you go to bed tonight
Think of the Fishing people as they surveyed their plight
And they watched as dead fish bloated
And they watched as dead birds floated
And silently they noted
That disaster had struck in the night

Think of the Tisza River as you slip between the sheets
Think of deserted villages and of their empty streets
There's dark despair on the evil tide
As invisible poisons softly glide
In a stream polluted with cyanide
Tis the end of the local fleets

Think of the Tisza River before you go to sleep
Think of Cyanide in the mud penetrating deep
What of the Shannon? What of the Suir?
What of the Barrow? What of the Nore?

Is this what their future holds in store?
Think of the Tisza River then close your eyes and weep.

17 March, 2000

This spillage of Cyanide took place in the Tisza River which flows into the Danube. It was a disaster which made headlines, but then faded quickly from the Media

15

WHARF TALK

Hey Lads, go sell your tonnage
Let the Celtic Tiger roar
Many Motor Fishing Boats
Don't need it any more.
So if you're dredging mussels
Or harvesting the clam
You needn't Register that boat
So what if it’s a scam!

They stopped a little crabber
From fishing near the Hook
And the Navy caught a trawler here
For having no Log Book
Yet the Fleet is being added to
By boats with pots galore
Some have bogus numbers
That the Authorities ignore

Hey Lads, go sell your tonnage
To Hell with Rules and Regs.
You'll get three thousand pounds a tonne
(And more in Killybegs!)
But hurry, don't be left behind

And sell your tonnage quick
The Minister may change his mind
Then you'll look pretty sick.

Boats of 50ft and over which had apparently never done anything about the Code of Practice were given Bi valve licenses. The compliant people felt really sick about it

16

THE SHANAKEE
(The Old Man)

Every Fishing vessel
That sails from Dunmore East
Should have a "Shanakee" on board
Or a loan of one at least.

The weather kept us in from Sea
While the Nor West gale it blew
So we pulled warps along the Quay
They were sticky black and new

The old man said "I was splicing wire
On a ship of the Grey Funnel Line
The Sun overhead was a ball of fire
And the weather was awful fine"

Now we were in an awful rush
To finish and get our grub
To rid our hands of the tarry stuff
And get our selves up to the pub

But the old man started off anew
And pausing he said with a smile

"Below the Equator the Albatross flew
A gliding for mile after mile"

"We sailed" he said, "To the Gran do Sole
Across the Sargassy Sea
Where I loved a girl as black as coal
A ballerina called Fi – Fi

Her father had a mighty ranch
A million acres wide
He offered me my golden chance
And his daughter for my bride

Out there in the Tropic night
As I kissed my sweet Fi-fi
I promised her that I would write
But I couldn't speak the Portugee"

Well we jumped aboard and ate our stew
Delving with fork and spoon
Then we left him where the Albatross flew
And his Fi- Fi gazed at the moon.

The old – timer's stories were a great part of life on a trawler and although full of exaggeration (or pure invention) they were great fun and helped to pass the time.

"Grey Funnel Line" (slang) were British Royal Navy Ships.

17

SEA DOGS

The worst of times we soon forget
The roly days, the cold and wet
Or damaged gear hauled on the Pier
And the never ending mending net
Counting meshes, get it right
Measure bridles, haul 'em tight
There's teamwork here, camaraderie
We warm our hands on mugs of tea.

Then its time for yarning
For laughing at the jokes
For kicking off the oilers
For lighting up the smokes.
It's a time before we go to sleep
Time for closing tired eyes
It's a time when toilers of the deep
Tend to philosophise.

"Do ye ever think of dying Skipps.
And wonder where ye'll go?"
"To Heaven of course ya stupid gits!"
"Yeah more like down below!"
"About Reincarnation

Now that's the job for me
I'll come back as an alsation
Before I'd choose the Sea!"

18

GIGANTIC DAWN

They named her the Gigantic Dawn
But seeing our stocks nearly gone
The owners took a sudden notion
To send her to the Indian Ocean

So will the native Fishers
In the island of Mauritius
Express their heartfelt gratitude
That a vessel of such magnitude
Will lend a hand in finishing
Their stocks which are diminishing?

There are livelihoods attainable
Let us leave what is sustainable
To the families who are fishing
In that sensible tradition
Which doesn't pose a threat
Like the Dawn's gigantic net

Must we catch fish by the million?
Process fillets by the billion?
I can't applaud these super ships
No Sardinella with my chips!

19

WILDLIFE

Among endangered species
Is the Lesser-Spotted Crew
Around our Coast some years ago
They numbered quite a few
You would see them at the mackerel
Or at the salmon nets
When domesticated
They were often kept as pets

Their life was never easy
And they got some awful teasing
To be addressed as "Pizza face"
Mustn't have been pleasing
How they suffered in the small boats
From sea sickness and cold
But that is where they learned the ropes
And they did as they were told

They were the backbone of the fishing fleet
That's where its future lay
But they somehow got neglected
By the Government of the day
No kids to hold the nets now

And to have a go at mending
No boy to say, "Can I steer her dad?"
As the fishing trip is ending

No the Lesser Spotted Crewman
Has lost its habitat
The small boat fleet is vanishing
And that's the end of that.

More Youngsters are leaving to work ashore. Soon there will be only we Grey Heads left.

20

EIGHT METRE MICKEY

This is the tale of Mickey Mac
And of his cousin Willy Strong
Mick did building "on the Black"
And fished a boat Eight metres long.

Now Willy fished with pots and line
And never ever drew the Dole
His boat was only five point nine
That poor misguided simple soul

Alone he faced the winter seas
While Mick's boat lay tied up in port
And Mick made money at his ease
And naturally was never caught

The days got short, the weather worse
And men like Willy couldn't earn
The Minister opened up his purse
So deeply felt was his concern

But did the Minister decide
And was it really his intent

That Eight-Metre Mickey qualified
While Willy could not pay his rent?

The Minister, in his wisdom gave a financial aid package to fishing vessels due to the extremely harsh winter. Great news but for the smaller boats below eight metres which didn't qualify though of course they needed it most.

21

OLD SHANOON

The Skyline is changing in Dunmore East
They're digging and ripping up old Shanoon
They might have got Planning Permission at least
Before making it look like the face of the moon
But don't be too sad
And don't be too sorry
It can't be all bad
We have gained a new quarry
Now half of Shanoon's
Gone away on a lorry.

12 December 2000

An amazing burst of activity on the HEADLAND while our workplace just below falls apart.

22

ENLARGEMENT

Will you be tying up your boat
While you're going up to vote
To say "yes" to the Treaty of Nice?
While they have the temerity
To claim it means prosperity
And an absolute necessity for peace!

But its about a Super state that the Europeans gain
And its to help the fattest cats get even fatter
Its so Poland's fishing fleet can join the boats of Spain
With the Baltic Fleet entirely, for that matter

Now with grim determination
They seek approval from the Nation
As even now they're mounting their campaign
But if they lose the referendum
They will take the Rules and bend 'um
And wait awhile then try it on again.

23

STAND UP AND BE COUNTED

Oh Eamon You're an awful man
Letting conscience rule your head
You should have voted "Yes" to Nice
But you voted "No" instead

Some colleagues were astounded
When they heard you did confess
Commissioners were confounded
You've put Brussels in a mess

Now your felony's compounded
By admitting to the Press
That concerned for Irish sovereignty
You hadn't voted "Yes"

So if the Cabinet be re- shuffled
Some Fisher folk are wishing
That instead of being muffled
They'll make you Minister for Fishing

A Government Minister with a conscience!

24

HAPPY MOTORING

All day I'm in my Garage
Selling cars and motor spares
It's a job you might disparage
With its worries and its cares

But at five o'clock I'm down the Dock
Then away out on the Briny
In my thirty foot half - decker
With its engine new and shiny

She needs no numbers on her bow
To catch mackerel after tea
No need for buying tonnage now
Its my hobby don't you see?

And the week - ends hauling tangle nets?
To you this might sound funny
Its harmless the bit of fish we gets
And we certainly don't make money

You seldom see us landing stuff
You might say its just a nixer!
And we don't be out there when it is rough
'Cos I'm a Motor Vehicle Fixer.

25

AGAINST THE ODDS

Pronsias was a Fisherman bold
He smelled of salt and diesel
Nuala thought him weird and old
With his features like a weasel
But he gazed into her big blue eyes
And he told her quite convincing lies
And gently stroked her steaming thighs
Then rolled her in the buttercups and teasel.

26

Away With the Fairies

E. U. Commissioner Riddle-me-ree
What is the point of your failed C.F.P.?
What does it conserve
And who do we serve
By throwing dead Codfish back in the sea?

Ireland is allowed to catch a tiny quota of fish in its own waters. French and Spanish Fishermen have a massive allowance of fish in the same area. They can laugh at the Irish who have to dump any fish over this paltry quota that they catch.

27

FOOTPRINTS

The Celtic Tiger is keeling o'er
Like a weak and sickly pup
So what will happen to Old Dunmore
Now the harbour's silting up?

There is a cost to the Industry
With silting and congestion
The trouble is the Powers that be
Aren't open to suggestion

The Fishermen do their very best
Coping with poor facilities
Do we have to put them to the test
And challenge their abilities

The boats are going hard aground
When they come to land their herrings
And rubbish wraps their props around
And ruins shafts and bearings

But dredging does cost money
And there was some set aside

And though this might sound funny
It went West upon the tide

The Tiger's footprints marked the sand
But Dunmore missed his bounty
It seems they live in "No Man's Land"
Down South in Waterford County.

Zero Investment!

28

A JOB FOR LIFE

I am a Sellafield Worker and you must understand
That everything in Sellafield is absolutely grand
Though we do admit there was a bit
Of confusion in the past
That's years ago and its afterglow
Was not expected to last

We Workers are safe in our spaceman suits
When the pipe work leaks, sure it never pollutes
And it won't get into our vulcanised boots
Unless through a very small hole

So don't you hurry when the siren wails
And don't you worry when the system fails
When the warning gauges go off the scales
'Cos everything's under control

I sleep easy at night and I never take fright
With a Geiger - counter under me bed
I wear lead lined jocks and to guard me from
shocks
I have the blankets pulled over me head.

After a leak at Sellafield!

29

IN THE NATIONAL INTEREST

They called her the "Mobile Gurrier"
She has a fifteen bladed screw
Every modern inconvenience
And a multi - national crew

The hull was built in Norway
And the engine in Japan
The Cookie comes from Galway
And the Mate from Pakistan

The Skipper's a Turk called Patsy
And among the Millionaire backers
Is one absconding Nazi
And two Romanian Knackers

It's nice to see she's doing well
Helping catch the Irish Quota
The price of tonnage has gone to hell
But who cares one iota?

06/05/02

Big ships built elsewhere, crewed by non Irish, non EU and often inexperienced people contribute nothing to the Industry or to the coastal community.

30

THE FLOATING VOTER

I am a Small - boat Fisherman
You must think me an Ass
I am really unimportant
A Citizen Second Class

I am fed up with those promises
That don't materialise
There's nothing for the Small – boat man
Its all for bigger guys

I've no time for Politicians
By now that must be plain
So if they call a Referendum
And Nice comes up again
Then I will vote against 'em
And let you do the same

Damn the European Parliament
And Damn their C.F.P.s
Damn their old enlargement
Just give us back our Seas.

31

AN IRISH NIGHTMARE

I had a dream, the funniest dream
The Good Ship "Leeson Lane" had been demolished
And in my dream, with a puff of steam
The Department of Marine had been abolished

The Mandarins were rescued from the waves
By the Fishermen with whom they had been fighting
Who then treated them like humble galley slaves
And put them tailing prawns and gutting whiting

Oh such weeping when they faced a life of fishing
It meant weeks without their sweethearts and their wives
How they pleaded when they said that they were wishing
To return again to living carefree lives

Well, I rolled out of the bunk and I turned the radio on
To hear the announcer's voice all deep with sorrow

Saying "I'm sorry to convey that your Minister has gone
And his Departments going to get the chop tomorrow!"

11/06/02

The Taosieach forgot to appoint a Minister for the Marine and Fisheries. After a while he did stitch together "The Department of the Marine, Communications and Natural Resources".

32

JUNK MAIL

Pat the Postie delivered the Packet
As I met him at my door
I said "Hold on Matey, what's the racket?
What are these fancy tablets for?"

He said
"Don't you worry if Sellafield blows up
With Iodine tablets bung your nose up!"
I said
"Thank you Pat that sounds real nice
Do the Powers – that – be give us more advice?

He said
"Now listen well and remember this
'Tis fatal to leave any orifice
Open to wind and radiation
And short term pain might be your salvation"

I said
"Yah –boo! Our Political Masters
Haven't a clue on Nuclear Disasters"
Well Pat jumped into his Post Office van
Yelling, "That pill is in the Emergency Plan

Its being tested and the latest story
Is to use it as a suppository!"

24/06/02

The Emergency Plan launched with great fanfare and enormous expense, ensured that every household received a pack of Iodine tablets as a protection against a Chernobyl type accident. It has all since been forgotten about!

33

NICE ONE

I think about Nice and I'd like to be nice
I'm a fisherman with a small boat
So on this occasion I need some advice
Please tell me, what way should I vote?

The last Referendum had me confused
Voting "No" just like the majority
As was only right I was soundly abused
And told "Yes" should have been my priority

So if I am nice about Nice and vote "Yes"
Will things be improving for me
Will Ireland sort out its Licensing mess
And Brussels remove C.F.P.?

06/07/02

34

ET TU BONO

Hey Bono, go sing for your supper
And leave the Nice Treaty aside
That "No" vote's not easy to scupper
And the Irish alone will decide.

It is well you don't fish for a living
But instead croon a fal-de-ral-day
Perhaps you would be less forgiving
If they traded your living away!

26/07/02

He campaigned for a "Yes" vote! If he lived here AND paid all his taxes here we'd think more of him.

35

A LETTER TO THE MINISTER

To The Minister of Communications,
The Marine And Other Lost Causes.

This boat is a whore to roll and pitch
With thirty pots inside
With low horse- power she's a perfect bitch
She will hardly punch the tide

Now I need a boat that's bigger
It is not to catch more fish
I'm not wanting a twin rigger
Only safety is my wish

But tonnage has gone awful dear
And we just can't compete
Tho' it isn't us that over fish
And cause stocks to deplete

So Minister do your best for me
While I'll not grovel and fawn
If you're sympathetic to my plea
I'll call her "Atlantic Prawn"

20/08/02

36

DEMOCRACY RULES

I voted "No" in the first Referendum
Europrats think that's most unkind
They take our rules and just up-endum
Because they want the Nice treaty signed

Now they try to hare-um scare-um
But here is something they will find
Telling stories quite horrendum
Ain't gonna make me change my mind

37

COMING HOME TO ROOST

I always vote and let me tell you why
It's in case the margins do be awful narrow
Then straight and true my single vote will fly
To find its destination like an arrow
And neatly targeting some Politician's seat
It may dislodge him like a dull and dusty sparrow
Who'd masqueraded as a shining Parakeet
And hid from us the truth about tomorrow.

January '03

I want to be like Mugabe's supporters "Vote early and vote often!"

38

WHO IS HE CODDING?

Fischler loves me this I know
Because the TV tells me so.
He loves Ireland's sea and rocks
He loves our Cod and our Monkfish stocks
With Spaniards let in the Irish box
He's as welcome as a dose of pox.

Fisheries Commissioner Franz Fischler plans to visit Ireland

39

CALL ME COCO

Isn't it great?
Isn't it sweet?
They're giving free tonnage to the whole Irish fleet
Bring on the clowns
Oh where are the clowns?

Isn't it great?
Isn't it grand?
You'll get a license free into your hand
Bring in the clowns
There have to be clowns

Isn't it sweet?
Isn't it great?
I've just bought ten tons at the premium rate
Where are the clowns
There have to be clowns

Don't worry we're here!

25/03/03

An extra three thousand Tons are wheedled out of the EU by the Government "To assist the small boat sector" i.e. to facilitate those who despite being given several opportunities, did nothing at all about getting themselves legally registered.

40

MUDDY WATERS

Through narrow lanes I wander
On my little fifty Honda
As stars grow paler with the coming day
Then I descend the Harbour Hill
To where our boats lie quiet and still
And where the Lighthouse casts its beam across the Bay

Then I climb aboard the boat
And pull on my oilskin coat
And my rubber boots to keep my feet from wilting
But imagine my surprise
When I find I'm high and dry
And it's all because the Dunmore Harbour's silting

Now they can dredge the River Suir
Half a million tonnes or more
And dump it on our doorstep – that's just fine
But it really makes me wonder
If the Authorities up yonder
Have ever cared a jot for me and mine

As the fishing grounds get covered
And the tiny fish get smothered
And Lobsters lose their natural habitat
I think that you will find
That “out of sight is out of mind”
And fishermen don’t count so that is that!

30/08/03

Deeper gets the mud!

41

TEARS OF COMFORT

The suit was grey and very neat
His shirt and tie of matching hues
Immaculate from head to feet
He wore those nice Italian shoes

And when the introduction was completed
He listened and he noted our complaints

Then explained to those around the table seated
How delays were due to budget'ry constraints

"However things are moving" he concluded
We thought him "fair enough" and without guile
He said "improvements to your harbour are
 included
But we perceived a tiny crocodilian smile

So times gone by yet nothings been achieved
Though faithfully he meets us once a year
To tell the truth we never were deceived
By words of comfort and a crocodile's tear.

15/03/04

42

AN EXACT SCIENCE

Now setting nets is quite an art
You can get it off a computer
But if you want to catch the Cod
Then you have to be much cuter

Are your trawl doors working right?
Does your foot line need more tension?
Have you measured your top sheet?
And do your bridles need attention?

If you can't answer "No" or "Yes"
To these and other questions
Then you are surely in a mess
But here are some suggestions

Buy yourself a modern net
One with a bit of height
Find a good Cod Fisherman
And have him set it right

So, ye Scientists and Boffins all
Come quickly to your senses

Because you can't use a proper trawl
We suffer the consequences.

01/03/04

Scientists using outmoded gear and with limited experience and very few fishing days draw the wrong conclusions. Most of the time they rely on other people's previous surveys and "guestimates".

43

DUBLIN WE LUV YA

Now I am a Civil Servant
I am faithful and subservient
I dot my Is and always cross my Ts
But that word "Decentralisation"
Is a curse upon the Nation
And will bring the Marine department to its
 knees.

Don't send me down to Cavan Town
Where cows do ruminate
Where Colleens diggin' ditches
Wearing britches congregate

CLONAKILTY. ANNUAL DRISHEEN HARVEST

Don't bury me in Clonakilty
Where the drisheen grows on trees
And the pudding factory chimneys
Pour black smoke upon the breeze.

Oh Minister take pity
My wife is going wild
Just leave us in Our City
Cork's no place to raise a child!

26/07/04

Should have sent them to Spitzbergen

44

A GREAT RESOURCE

Silver and Gold. You remember me?
I am the Herring. King of the Sea
Exported to Holland and High Germany
Once your Paymaster
I'm now a disaster
Reduced to Fishmeal in a big factory.

With prices for Herring right down on the floor
Depletion of stocks you would have to deplore
Not good for the Trawlers not good for Dunmore
To earn that distinction
You fished to extinction
The Silver and Gold that wont come anymore.

21/10/04

How did we mange to get it so wrong?

45

THIS IS PLAN "B"

We are the Marine Surveyors
You might meet us on the Quay
We are the scourge of Fishermen
Yet we never go to Sea

We have certificates in frames
Hanging on our office wall
And there are letters behind our names
Just to prove to one and all
We knows it all. We knows it all

So the Da taught you to fish
To gauge the weather and the tide?
Well very soon you're going to wish
That you'd been qualified

Then you could be a Surveyor
We mean a real Marine Surveyor
A really keen Marine Surveyor
A really mean Marine Surveyor

Then you'd agree our Plan is neat
To just reduce the small boat fleet

Til its destruction is complete
For our criteria they can't meet
Our Code of Practice has them beat
Its very neat. So very neat.

18/01/05

Some of these guys knew nothing at all about Fishing and fishing boats. One we know of has never even been to sea! Some of these have been appointed by the Department to oversee the "Code of Practice". If you get a wrong 'un it can cost you a bundle!

46

A MOTHER'S WISH

Come here to me my bonny son
You are the one
My currant bun
You've been to school
You're not a fool
What will you do for your career?
Stay off the beer
Your Mammy's here
With sound advice
Won't it be nice?
Think of the money and the fame
Think what you'll gain
What you'll attain
You've got my brain
We're good at books
You've inherited your Dad's good looks
He's just a slob
He's ne'er a bob
Just boats and nets
And heaps of debts
You say you want to join him at the fishing?
You're like the rest
A blasted pest

Off with you then
Now that you're ten
Put on your boots and go and earn a living!

07/03/05

Recalling the happier times when kids ran away from school to join in our Great Adventure (much to their Mammy's disapproval).

47

BOGMEN BEWARE

The Mandarins of Leeson Lane
Have gone and got it wrong again
The Scallop Fishing's down the drain
And Wexford families feel the pain
We all agree that it's a shame
The people ask "Who is to blame?"
Well it's each rotating Minister
Who though meaning nothing sinister
Has simply handed over power
To a certain unelected shower
Who dwell within their Ivory Tower
In Dublin's Leeson Lane

Before all is lost I can't help wishing
The Mandarins would leave the Fishing
And before our Industry's quite dead
Go administer our Bogs instead.

10/06/05

Some of the Kilmore Quay Scallop Dredgers suddenly find their Bi valve licence is no longer allowing them to fish.

48

HEALTHCARE

Come gather round ye fisher lads
And hear my tale of woe
It concerns Old Hairy Mad Magrew
Who blew in long ago
He blew in with that Easterly wind
The one they call Sirocco
He blew in from some foreign land
Either Cornwall or Morocco
He arrived upon the Irish shore
On a day both dull and foggy
And in accent strange to Irish ears
He shouted "Oggy! Oggy!"
But the Village took him to its heart
And kept him fed and watered
And they rented him a chicken house
Where he was snugly quartered

Well his luck held good for many a year
As he fished his little boat
Until when jigging mackerel
The lead went down his throat
That lead went down his throat me boys
A three pound mackerel lead

He thought "I'd better get ashore
Or else I'll soon be dead"
So he quickly headed back to port
For medical assistance
With his engine doing a thousand revs
He soon reduced the distance
He called the Rescue Services
He sent "Pan Pan Medico"
The ambulance stood on the Pier
Warmed up and set to go

By the time he entered harbour
Hairy's eyes were wide with fear
So Eddie used the fork lift truck
To hoist him on the Pier
Then they whisked him off to Waterford
To Ardkeen's A and E
With a label on his stretcher
Stating "Accident at Sea"
Now Hairy he felt safe at last
But he'd not anticipated
That swallowing a mackerel lead
Would leave him constipated
And all that week he'd ample time
To contemplate his folly
Alas alack he was on his back
Upon a hospital trolley

Now Hairy feared the doctors
But was sweet on young nurse Capple
And he said "Fair Miss I'll give you a kiss

If you get me a big green apple"
Being young and innocent
She responded to his wheedling
By hopping over the garden wall
And nicking a Brambly Seedling
When the apple came
He was ahead of the game
And swallowed the darn thing whole
Then he instantly flew to the outpatient's loo
And made for the toilet bowl

To everyone's shock he destroyed the whole block
The experience left him nigh dead
But when news circulated he was soon fumigated
And tucked in a hospital bed
It was all a disgrace but they wouldn't lose face
The consultant was shaking his head
"But for our diagnosis he'd contract the Osmosis
And finish up terribly dead
We have no Statistics on handling Ballistics
So call in the army instead!"

So remember Hairy suffering there
When you go jigging have a care
Forget the Code of Practice crap
When hauling mackerel shut your trap.

28/03/05

"Oggy" slang for a Cornish Pasty. "Oggy! Oggy!" At full volume is the battle cry of the Cornish Rugby team.

FOGBOUND

ANOTHER BLOW-IN MAKES A LANDFALL

49

THE BALLAD OF B. A. CUTEHOOR

Thank you very much for the Derogation
This time the Minister's dropped a clanger
I've another year without Registration
Although this boat is a woeful banger

Her propeller's fairly gobbled
And her steering is only hanging
Her exhaust pipe has been cobbled
I think that's what makes the banging

You've all had your boats Surveyed
And these Surveyors are expensive
You're short of cash now they've been paid
'Cos their demands are quite extensive

The Safety Standards must be met
Before they let you off to sea
So now you end up deep in debt
But no not me says I, not me

Thank you very much for the Derogation
Let Fishermen round the Coast complain

I'm much amused at their Frustration
While I'm still fishing for profit and gain

P.S. And fair play to me!

17/08/05

The Minister gives more time to some of those who never did anything towards registering their boats.

50

THE FOUR SEASONS
Or a Hundred Thousand Phone Calls

Spring
Hello Dermot! Hello Lisa!
Remember me?
I am that poor misguided Geezer
Who once applied for
Boat's Registration
As is required by the laws within our Nation.

Summer
I sent my Blue form
But you can't trace it
That screws my Application, so let's face it
I am not greedy
I'm not a grabber
I just need to fish my seven metre crabber

Autumn
Hello Damien! Hello James Dear!
It's so nice now
We are using our first names here
We are a long time

Upon this Mission
But I really need to do some serious fishin'.

Winter
Hello Dermot! Hello Lisa!
This Code of Practice
Well it is a proper teaser
And it cost more
Than I reckoned
Merry Christmas! Bye-the-way this is our Second!

15/10/05

Registering a fishing boat one gets on first name terms with a lot of people in The department of the Marine. Dermot, Damien, James and Lisa are real people who all had a hand in processing the registration and licensing of my boat. There were others too who remained mere acquaintances!

51

GHOSTS OF CHRISTMAS PAST

The sea was a wobbly green jelly
The sun was a pale custard pie
I'd a pain in me head an' me belly
And I wanted to lie down and die

Last night we were out making merry
T'was Christmas or was it New Year?
There was Dan Joe and Stocky from Kerry
And Pee Jay from Castletownbere.

Enjoying the craic was young Jimmy Black
And O'Driscolls from near Ballyshannon
And from Ballyhack came Paddy and Jack
And Willie who came from Duncannon

Well this Christmas came and I was still game
For dancing the jig and the reel
But it's really a shame and I'm not to blame
For feeling the way that I feel

'Cos the sea is a wobbly green jelly
And the sun is a pale custard pie
And if we get herring this evening
I swear that I'll lie down and die!

52

THE LAND OF SINKING BOLLARDS

If you go down to the Dock today
Beware of little men.
They range in height from four foot eight
To almost five foot ten.

They wear fluorescent waistcoats
And helmets white or blue.
And the magic spells they weave
Can spell the end for me and you.

Oh we have heard them chanting
Their strange satanic verse.
Crying Spirit level, Plumb bob,
Theodolite and worse.

Then they mixed a magic potion
And they poured it on the Quays.
And though some went in the Ocean
It still came to their knees.

So if you don't believe me
Go and look at what they've done.

They half-buried Dunmore's Bollards
They have done in every one.

28/12/08

A lot of money spent re surfacing the East Pier which didn't help us one bit!

53

THE LISBON PILGRIMAGE

The way up to the polling booth
Will be painful, long and slow
For I shall walk it barefoot
Or at least I'll have a go
And if I feel defeated
In hail, or rain or snow
Or if my feet are blistered
And bleeding, heel and toe
Then I will crawl on hands-and-knees
And I'll still be voting "NO"!

30/01/09

The SECOND run of the Lisbon Treaty (See Nice Treaty etc.)

54

RAISING THE ASGARD
Or Procrastination Pays for Itself

The Greens' concern for insects can only be
 admired
The Fianna Fail led Government is equally
 inspired
By a little chap who does his work without
 complaint or quibble
By eating wrecks, both hulls and decks.
I mean of course, the Gribble.

He's just a little wormy thing that lives beneath
 the sea
He munches any kind of wood from every type of
 tree,
He'll start with Larch or Douglas fir beneath the
 water-line
And eat for main course frames of Oak
And that will do him fine.

He also never dines alone but brings along his
 mates
And there's not much left of a shipwreck when
 they all participates.

So a million munching gribbles fulfil our
  Government's wish
As the Asgard stays on the seabed
And becomes their favourite dish.

So let us have a Survey at the tax-payers expense
Then the Minister can tell us, that her salvage
  makes no sense
Because the "As" has gone out of Asgard, and we
  really do regret it
But Gribbles, them little wormy things,
Have been and gone and ate it.

17/06/09

The disgraceful abandonment of the beautiful National Treasure, the Tall Ship Asgard.

TIMBER CONSUMING GRIBBLE
(ONE TENTH ACTUAL SIZE)

55

NAVIGATIONAL WARNING
Or Death of a Fishing Port

If you fish the South Coast
Then beware of Dunmore East
For waiting in the Harbour
There is a terrifying Beast

The Forty-legged Quango
Lies waiting in its lair
Within the Harbour Master's House
So approach it with due care

For you are being monitored
And recorded on a tape
Once the Quango gets its claws in you
There will be no escape

The S.F.P.A. will get you
That Beast with forty legs
So head away for Kilmore Quay
Or even Killybegs

If you've made a log book error
Retained a bass or river eel

You'll get a criminal record
And there will be no appeal

So give her welly Skipper
Head for another Port
Better burn a lot more diesel
Than face a trip to court.

10/03/10

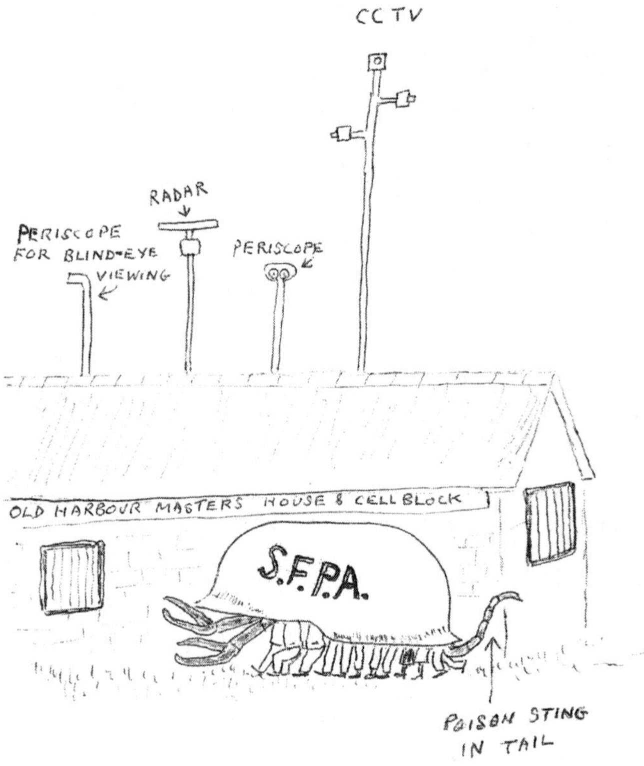

56

FAREWELL AND ADIEU.
To the Bail-out Boys

Get you gone, you Ministers of Transport, Marine
  and Tourism.
Now reap the benefits of those years of cute
  hoorism.
And though still young or in your middle years
Enjoy your tax free pensions safe from any fears
Of swingeing cuts, as suffered by the Aged, Infirm
  and Blind,
Inflicted by your Party in a manner most unkind
Supported by those perfidious, insect-hugging
  Greens
Along with the-Minister-without-a-mandate
Our Hospitals' Queen-of-Queens.

Don't you dare speak to us of job creation
Or of putting first the interest of the Nation
What of our Fishermen and their job retention?
Whilst all of you signed away our great resource
So leaving many of our lads with no recourse
But to seek employment in a distant land.

Aye Ministers off with you now and with your
  pockets
Stuffed with cash
The time has come for you to make your final
Farewell dash
To your Villa in the balmy Cote d'Azure
And let us bid you all "fond Goodbye and Adieu
At our expense and may you long enjoy the craic
You may rest assured that we will never, EVER ask
  you back.

57

THE DISAPPEARED

Our Harbour Master's gorn away
Some said he'd fled to Stornaway
While others with "the inside track"
Said he'd bought a shack near Ballyhack
Where e'er he's gone we wish him well
That Elusive Maritime Pimpernel.

In an earlier period, our Harbour Master suddenly left and we had to struggle on without one!

Limpet Lodge,
Dunmore East,
Co. Waterford.

27 May, 2002

Tom MacSweeney,
Seascapes,
R.T.E.
Cork.

Dear Tom,

I heard the poem "The Qualified Man" on Seascapes performed excellently (by Gerri I think). Cranpole heard it too as was obvious from his demeanour. All week he was swanning around, spouting bits of Shakespeare etc. after the style of some famous actor or something. He is some poser alright! He even took to wearing a big floppy plum coloured velvet beret. Stupid and embarrassing really.

Anyway, I was in the shop overlooking the Harbour, when he came in. We had a whole SE gale at the time. Suddenly the door flew open and he just stood there with the rain swirling in around him. "Dramatic Entrance" I noted with a yawn. From behind the counter the comely Noleen yelled, " Shut the door! Are you trying to wash us out of it?" Cranpole ignored her request, strode up to the counter and in a voice a bit like the late great MacLiamor declaimed "Shall I compare thee to a summer's day?"

"Ger outa that!" She replied, fetching him a swipe across the chops, which would have knocked his silly hat flying had it not been for the green mending twine under his chin securing it against the tempest.

He quickly recovered his composure however and in his normal weaselly voice said, "OK well give me a ham and cheese sandwich and two sets of mackerel feathers then."

Thank you for the cheque. I cashed it and hid it away. If he once saw the colour of money there'd be no holding him. He'd want to give up the fishing and turn professional. Then what would become of us?

Thank you again Tom.

Yours etc,

Pandora xxx

Pandora

SHALL I COMPARE THEE TO A SUMMERS DAY?
YOU WHA'?
ANTI FOULING 2ND HAND
FISHING NEWS OUTRAGE!
RINE TIMES SHOCK!
RISH SKIPPER HORROR!